The Wild Outdoors

GO SKIING!

by
Heather Bode

Published by Capstone Press, an imprint of Capstone
1710 Roe Crest Drive, North Mankato, Minnesota 56003
capstonepub.com

**Library of Congress Cataloging-in-Publication Data is available on
the Library of Congress website.**
ISBN 9781666345841 (hardcover)
ISBN 9781666345858 (paperback)
ISBN 9781666345865 (eBook PDF)

Summary: Readers learn about the proper clothing, footwear, and
supplies needed for both downhill and cross-country skiing. Text and
full-color photographs describe how to stay safe and have fun while
taking part in a popular winter sport.

Image Credits
Getty Images: clu, 8, David Madison, 29, Erik Isakson, 15,
JordanSiemens, 20, stockstudioX, 27, ZU_09, 7; Shutterstock:
Alexandre Rotenberg, 21, anatoliy_gleb, 14, BearFotos, 19, Cascade
Creatives, 25, gorillaimages, Cover, l i g h t p o e t, 11, my nordic, 23,
nics_coles, 5, nikolpetr, 16, Sergey Novikov, 1, 24, smereka, 13, Stock
Up, 18, Tatiana Popova, 9, tomtsya, 17, wassiliy-architect, 10

Editorial Credits
Editor: Erika L. Shores; Designer: Dina Her; Media Researchers:
Jo Miller and Pam Mitsakos; Production Specialist: Tori Abraham

All internet sites appearing in back matter were available and accurate
when this book was sent to press.

Table of Contents

Words in **bold** are in the glossary.

GET SCHOOLED IN SKIING

The wind howls. A chill goes through your body. Bright snow blankets the backyard. It can be hard to play outside in winter. There is an activity you can do that makes you move fast. It warms your body and is fun and exciting at the same time. Some scientists believe it may even make you smarter. What is it? Skiing!

Skiing builds problem-solving, planning, and concentration skills that can help you in school. Skiing also builds **coordination** and improves your ability to move. You will be surrounded by beautiful scenery, fresh air, and tons of sparkling, white snow. Skiing may take you to places you have never seen before. Or you might see a familiar place in a new way while you enjoy the wintery outdoors.

Skiing uses both brain and muscle power as you glide over the snow.

Chapter 1

ANCIENT ORIGINS

Who invented skiing? Nobody knows for sure. Ancient cave paintings in China show hunters on skis surrounding wild animals. The **Indigenous** people of Norway have a history of hunting and racing on skis that goes back thousands of years. Skiing was a way of transportation. People used skis for everyday tasks, such as getting to the next village, tending livestock, or going to the market.

Skis were originally made of pieces of flat wood. Fur or horsehair on the bottom provided some grip. Wooden ski poles were used to balance and to help make turns. Toes of the boot were attached to the ski, but the heel was kept unattached. This allowed skiers to glide on flat land or climb uphill.

Hunters used skis to move quickly over the snow in winter.

Skis allowed people living in snowy parts of North America to travel more quickly than on foot.

Skiing was brought to North America by people who moved there from countries like Norway and Sweden. When they colonized new snowy regions, they used skis to get work done. Mail carriers, miners, hunters, and railroad workers used skis. Other workers used snowshoes. They noticed skis allowed them to cover longer distances in shorter amounts of time.

Over time, people realized skiing was just plain fun. Skis changed when the first mechanical ski lifts, also called chairlifts, were built in the 1930s. Ski lifts carried skiers to the mountaintop, so there was no need to keep heels free for climbing. A ski with a locked-in heel was created. This gave skiers better control when skiing down steep slopes. It also created two types of skiing: cross-country and downhill.

A ski lift takes downhill skiers to the top of a mountain.

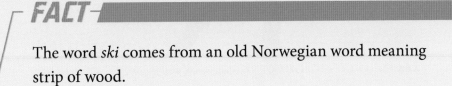

FACT

The word *ski* comes from an old Norwegian word meaning strip of wood.

Chapter 2

SKI SKILL: CROSS-COUNTRY

Cross-country skiing can be done on groomed trails. These are special trails made for skiing. Sometimes these trails are found at parks. No ski trails near you? You can try it in any big open space!

To go cross-country skiing, you need cross-country skis, poles, bindings, and ski boots. The bindings connect your boots to the skis at the toe. The ski boots look like shoes.

Some people compete in cross-country ski races.

Only the toe of the cross-country boot is attached to the ski.

It is important to dress in layers for cross-country skiing. You will want to wear several layers of clothes. The outer layer should be waterproof. Wear a winter hat and gloves. You can bring extras in case these get wet.

Cross-country skiing uses a kick-and-glide motion. You push off on one ski to glide on the other. Alternating this rhythm creates movement. Ski poles help you balance and provide **momentum** when pushing off on a ski.

Whether you are cross-country or downhill skiing, it is important to take a lesson from a trained ski instructor. They teach you the basics. Then you can practice on your own.

TIPS FOR BOTH TYPES OF SKIING:

- ☑ Finding your balance on skis is important. Skis move and your body must move along with them!
- ☑ Learning to "walk" in skis is a good place to start. Begin on a flat surface and see how your foot muscles react to keep your body upright. Some of your balance will depend on reflexes, or automatic movements your muscles make.
- ☑ Make sure to point your stomach in the direction you want to go before moving your feet.

A ski instructor shows a student how to turn.

Learning how to get back up after a fall is something every skier needs to practice.

Falling is a part of skiing. If you feel yourself falling, try to fall to the side. You can also crouch low and sit down in the snow. To get back up, roll yourself into a "dead bug" position. Lie on your back with your skis in the air. Then drop your legs to your side while keeping your skis **parallel**. Next roll over to your hands as if you are doing a push-up. "Walk" your hands on the snow toward your skis until you are standing. Of course, you can always take off one ski, stand up, and put it on again.

To stop or slow down, turn the tips of your skis inward. This creates a wedge, or snowplow, and will slow you down. Be careful not to cross the tips of your skis. This will make you lose control and fall.

A skier points the tips of their skis inward in the "snowplow" position.

FACT

Cross-country skiing requires more energy than downhill skiing. Cross-country trails are not as steep as downhill trails. You use more muscles to move your body over the snow.

Chapter 3

SKI SKILL: DOWNHILL

To downhill ski, you need to travel to a ski area or a ski resort. These are places where trails have been made. Both have ski shops where you can rent your equipment. Ski resorts are places where you can stay overnight. This way, you can ski for several days. A ski area does not have places to stay overnight.

A ski resort in the Alps mountain range in France

Wind blows snow around on a ski area in Norway.

Plan to go skiing on clear, sunny days. There will be less chance of snow and changing weather conditions. The sun shining means the temperature could be mild. You may need to consider the wind as well. Windy days feel much colder on your skin. The wind can also affect snow conditions.

Downhill ski equipment includes skis, a helmet, goggles, boots, and bindings. Downhill ski boots are very stiff. This helps support your ankles. Your heels will be locked to the skis. Goggles keep wind and snow out of your eyes. Sunlight reflecting off the snow is very bright.

Most downhill ski boots have two buckles across the toes and two buckles around the shin.

You may have to try out several pairs of boots and skis to find the right fit for you.

Most people rent ski equipment while they are learning. Skis and bindings come in different sizes. Workers at ski shops make sure your skis fit properly. You might be given ski poles. However, many ski instructors teach you to ski without poles. This way, you can focus on the movement of the skis and your balance. You will need to wear snow pants over your clothes, a winter coat, and gloves.

A skier going down the mountain shifts his weight to the right to turn.

To ski downhill, keep your skis parallel to each other. Shift your body's weight to the edges of the skis to turn. If you want to go right, shift your weight to the right on both feet. Keep your knees relaxed and slightly bent. Make a zigzag pattern as you go down the hill.

HOW TO RIDE A SKI LIFT:

- ☑ Look for a sign or a sticker on the ground that reads *Wait Here*.
- ☑ Put both ski poles in one hand and look back over your shoulder.
- ☑ When the chair comes, sit down and scoot to the back. To be safe, remain still while the lift is moving.
- ☑ As you near the top, keep the tips of your skis pointing up.
- ☑ Use your free hand to push yourself off the chair and slide away from the lift.

First-time skiers will need practice learning how to get on and off a ski lift.

Chapter 4

KNOW BEFORE YOU GO

Always be aware of the weather. In winter, snowstorms can move in quickly. Blowing snow can make it hard to see. Wearing sunscreen in winter might seem funny, but sunlight reflecting off snow can cause sunburn. Apply sunscreen to your neck and face.

It is important to keep your body covered with proper clothing. Frostbite can occur on fingers and toes. It looks like white or gray patches on the skin. It may not even hurt, but it is dangerous. Medical attention is needed. **Hypothermia** is when your body temperature lowers from being out in the cold. If you are shivering and you don't feel steady on your skis, it is time to go inside!

Skiers need waterproof and windproof clothing
if they plan to ski in harsh conditions.

Always ski with a buddy. You will have more fun. And if something unexpected happens, there will be someone there to help you.

Skiers must look out for any skiers who are ahead of them.

Keep your eyes looking forward so you can see what is happening ahead. Look out for other skiers and those who have fallen. You should always feel in control of your speed. If you cannot control your speed, you become a danger to others. Learning to ski is about balance and good technique instead of speed.

Ski trails are marked so that skiers know how difficult or easy they are.

Trails and Symbols

Each ski trail will have a color and symbol. Here is what they mean in North America:

easy trail   medium trail   harder trail   hardest trail

Chapter 5

SKIING AND THE ENVIRONMENT

Many people enjoy skiing, but some people fear it is hurting the environment. How? When ski resorts are built, trees must be cut down. This causes habitat loss for animals living there. Ski resorts and ski areas have snow machines to make snow. They need water to make snow. Sometimes this water comes from local lakes. This lowers the amount of water for the fish there.

People have also been noticing that the ski seasons are getting shorter. Temperatures on our planet are slowly warming. We call this climate change. This means snow conditions are not the same either. There may be fewer days of fresh, powdery snow.

Ski resorts and ski areas often have to use machines
to make enough snow for skiers to ski on.

Ski areas and resorts know they must work to protect the land from climate change. They are trying to cut back **carbon emissions** that lead to climate change. Carbon emissions come from burning coal, oil, and natural gas. Instead, ski resort owners are working to use **renewable energy** resources like solar power.

What can responsible skiers do? Ride in groups to ski areas. This saves gas and decreases traffic. Stay on the trails. Obey any posted signs. Make sure there is enough snow to be skiing. You should not see grass and other ground items sticking up through the snow. This ensures you are not harming the habitat.

Whether you try out cross-country skiing, downhill skiing, or both, it takes plenty of practice to improve your skills. But when next winter comes, you'll be excited to get outside and go skiing!

A cross-country skier uses a trail in the Sierra Nevada mountain range in the western United States.

GLOSSARY

carbon emission (KAHR-buhn ee-MISH-un)—the release of harmful gas into the air from machines and factories burning fossil fuels

coordination (koh-OR-duh-nay-shun)—the ability to control body movements

hypothermia (hye-puh-THUR-mee-uh)—when your body temperature falls below normal due to being out in the cold

Indigenous (in-DI-juh-nuhss)—the first people to live in a place

momentum (moh-MEN-tuhm)—the force or speed created by movement

parallel (PA-ruh-lel)—to be in a straight line and an equal distance apart

renewable energy (ri-NOO-uh-buhl EN-er-jee)—power from a source that does not get used up

READ MORE

George, Enzo. *Physical Science in Snow and Ice Sports.* New York: Crabtree Publishing Company, 2020.

Labrecque, Ellen. *Nordic Skiing.* Ann Arbor, MI: Cherry Lake Publishing, 2018.

Smith, Elliott. *Freeskiing and Other Extreme Snow Sports.* North Mankato, MN: Capstone, 2020.

INTERNET SITES

Kids on Lifts
kidsonlifts.org

Lids on Kids
lidsonkids.org

What Is Skiing?
rookieroad.com/skiing/what-is/

INDEX

ABOUT THE AUTHOR

Heather Bode is an elementary educator and author. She loves writing nonfiction she knows will be high-interest material for her students. Heather lives in Helena, Montana.